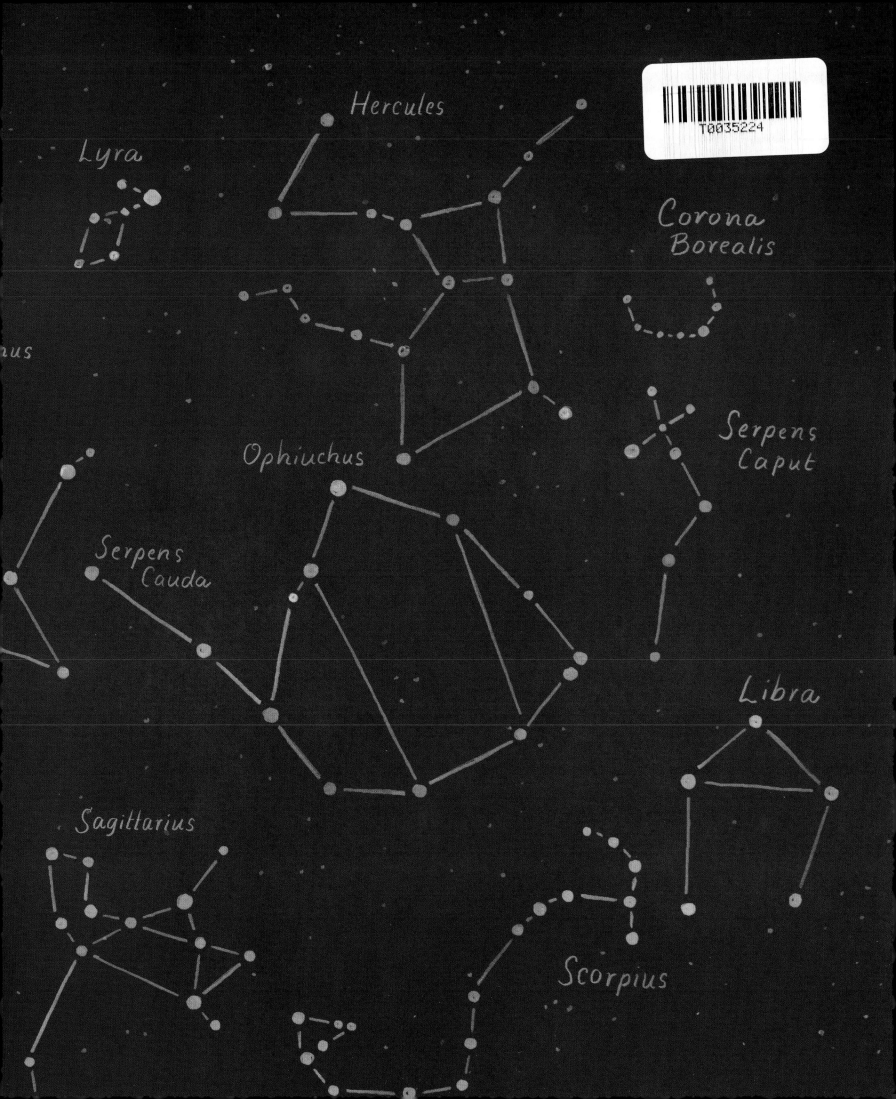

In loving memory of my father, Saul Blumenthal,
who lived life afire with learning —A.B.M.

To Ava —E.H.

Text copyright © 2019 by Alice B. McGinty
Jacket art and interior illustrations copyright © 2019 by Elizabeth Haidle

All rights reserved. Published in the United States by Schwartz & Wade Books, an imprint of Random House Children's Books,
a division of Penguin Random House LLC, New York.

Schwartz & Wade Books and the colophon are trademarks of Penguin Random House LLC.

Visit us on the Web! rhcbooks.com

Educators and librarians, for a variety of teaching tools, visit us at RHTeachersLibrarians.com

Library of Congress Cataloging-in-Publication Data is available upon request.
ISBN 978-1-5247-6831-7 (trade)
ISBN 978-1-5247-6832-4 (glb)
ISBN 978-1-5247-6833-1 (ebook)

The text of this book is set in Belen.
The illustrations were rendered in inks, in graphite powder, and digitally.

MANUFACTURED IN CHINA
4 6 8 10 9 7 5
First Edition

THE GIRL WHO NAMED
PLUTO

The Story of Venetia Burney

WRITTEN BY
Alice B. McGinty

ILLUSTRATED BY
Elizabeth Haidle

schwartz & wade books · new york

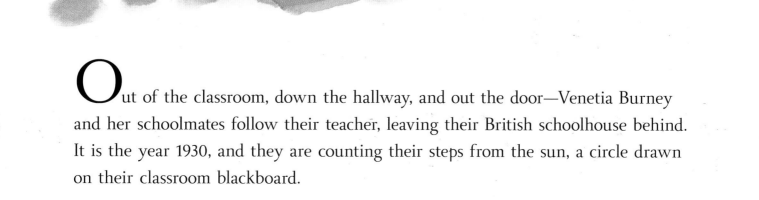

Out of the classroom, down the hallway, and out the door—Venetia Burney and her schoolmates follow their teacher, leaving their British schoolhouse behind. It is the year 1930, and they are counting their steps from the sun, a circle drawn on their classroom blackboard.

At exactly forty-one paces from the sun, they lay down a bird seed: Mercury.

At seventy-seven paces, they place a pea: Venus. Next, a larger pea: Earth.

After placing a bead for Mars and an orange for Jupiter, the largest planet, they stop at 1,019 paces, inside University Park. There, they lay down a golf ball: Saturn.

There are two more planets in the solar system, Uranus and Neptune, but Miss Claxton tells her students that they are too far away. She will let their imaginations finish the planet walk.

Saturn

Uranus

Neptune

1,019 paces from the sun

When Venetia and her friends return to the park later with lumps of clay for the planets, they run, counting paces to Mercury, Venus, Earth, Mars, Jupiter, Saturn . . . all the way to Neptune.

MARS

MERCURY

VENUS

EARTH

Venetia's imagination whirls, trying to fathom the real distances. She has memorized each number. Stormy blue Neptune orbits 2.79 billion miles from the sun. And what lies beyond? How far does the solar system reach?

Venetia brings her questions to breakfast each morning, and
Grandfather Madan answers as many as he can.

She and Mother have been living with Grandfather since Venetia's
father died. Old and stately like the Oxford library where he was
head librarian, Grandfather knows that questions lead to learning.
And his family is afire with learning.

Along with the planets, Venetia is learning about Greek and Roman gods. When she reads about Mars, the Roman god of war, she is reminded of her great-uncle, Henry Madan, a science master who named the two moons orbiting that planet. He chose Phobos and Deimos, Mars's twin sons. Moons and planets named from legends—what a marvelous link between science and story!

At breakfast one Friday, as Grandfather sifts through the newspaper, he starts to read aloud:

"A NEW PLANET: DISCOVERY BY LOWELL OBSERVATORY
Professor Harlow Shapley announced today that the Lowell Observatory at Flagstaff, Arizona, had discovered a ninth major planet. The planet, which has not yet been named, is beyond Neptune."

A new planet! Venetia leans forward in her chair. Another lump of clay to add to their model!

"I wonder what it should be called," Grandfather says, his brow creased.

Venetia's imagination takes off, flying, leaping, connecting the dots from science to story. She knows that this planet, so far from the sun, must be frozen, dark, and lifeless. It would be like the underworld— the underworld ruled in Roman myths by Neptune's brother, Pluto.

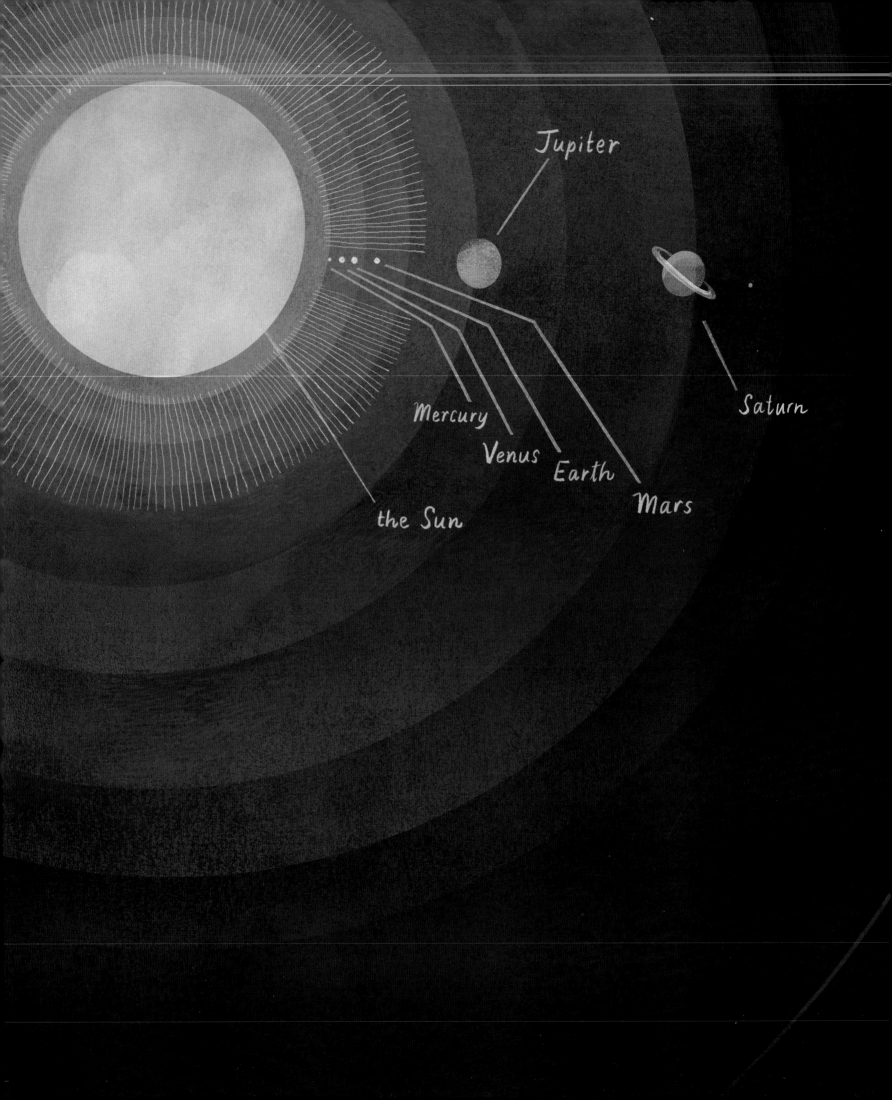

Jupiter

Mercury

Venus

Earth

Mars

Saturn

the Sun

Uranus

Neptune

"It might be called Pluto,"
Venetia says.

He tells Venetia that he'll share her idea with his friend,
Professor Herbert Hall Turner of the Royal Astronomical Society.
Perhaps he has a say in the decision.

After Venetia leaves for school, Grandfather writes this note:

On his way to the library, Grandfather drops off the note at the professor's home.

Meanwhile, not far away, Venetia and her schoolmates are buzzing with excitement about the new planet. They fire question after question at Miss Claxton.

Miss Claxton promises to find out.

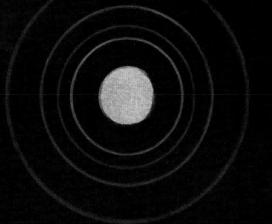

That evening, Venetia lies in bed, her mind adrift with Planet X. In the flurry of her thoughts spins one name: Pluto. Could it be the name for the new planet? Were the astronomers deciding now?

Saturday morning dawns, and Venetia and Grandfather
search the papers for more information about Planet X.
Mostly, though, they wait to hear from the professor.

That afternoon, a response arrives.

My dear Madan,
I got your note on my
return from London.
I think PLUTO excellent!
We did not manage to think
of anything so good at
the Royal Astronomical
Society yesterday.

THE ROYAL
ASTRONOMICAL
SOCIETY

The professor's note goes on to say that he has written to the
astronomers at Lowell about Pluto. It will be up to them to decide.

A week goes by.

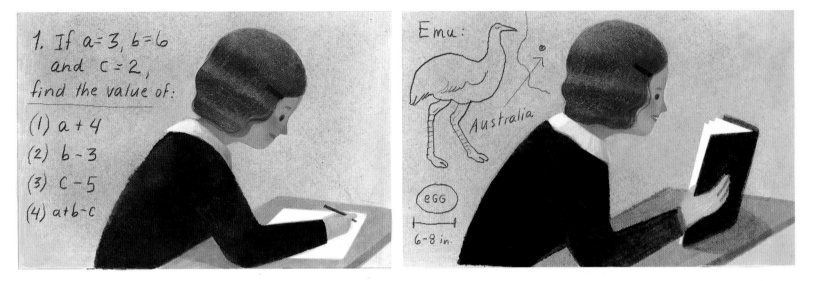

At school, Venetia works on lessons in math, science, and history.

At home, she and Grandfather keep busy—reading, playing,
and waiting. Will the astronomers like her idea?

March turns to April. And Venetia waits.

April drags on. Outside, the trees sprout leaves. And Venetia waits.

If Venetia could see what was happening across the ocean, she would find
that PLUTO has made its way through the doors of the Lowell Observatory
to Clyde Tombaugh, the shy assistant who discovered Planet X.

His first choice for a name? Pluto. Not only is it a perfect fit for this dark, icy world, but the first two letters are *PL*, the initials of astronomer Percival Lowell, who began the search for the planet.

Finally, at the end of the month, the astronomers vote.
It's unanimous. The ninth planet will be named Pluto.

When Grandfather shares the news with Venetia, she beams, her eyes radiant.

Grandfather sends a check to Miss Claxton, thanking her for her teaching. With the money, the school purchases a gramophone . . .

. . . and names it Pluto.

Venetia is a hero!

As Venetia grows, Pluto tilts and spins in its long, slow orbit around the sun. It shares the outer reaches of the solar system with other spheres newly discovered by astronomers.

Venetia gets older, and older still. Her hair turns silver.

And one gray July afternoon, the day before her eighty-ninth birthday, she
travels to the Observatory Science Centre, near the southern tip of England.
She has been invited to view Pluto through a telescope—her first time ever.

It's raining, though, and it takes a clear sky to see the dwarf planet.

But as Venetia nears, the rain stops and the clouds begin to part.

A lovely sunset fills the sky.

Later, the darkness twinkling with stars, Venetia and
the scientists climb to the observatory's dome, where
the 111-year-old telescope is waiting. The scientists locate
Pluto, and Venetia puts her eye to the lens.

"By God," she says in an awed voice. There it is, that icy sphere spinning 3.67 billion miles from the sun, many paces past Neptune—and its name is Pluto.

AUTHOR'S NOTE

VENETIA KATHARINE BURNEY was born in Oxford, England, on July 11, 1918. This book closely follows her true life story, including her planet walk at school, her great interest in studying the solar system  and Greek and Roman mythology, and her visit to the Observatory Science Centre when she was older. Venetia did indeed suggest the name Pluto after her grandfather shared the article about the planet's discovery, and the letters from Professor Turner and the astronomers' decision process about the name are historically accurate. When I put these events into the story, I imagined how Venetia waited, and how she reacted when she found out that her name, Pluto, had been chosen.

What happened to Venetia in the years after she named Pluto? She grew up to become an accountant, working with numbers, and later a math and economics teacher, pursuing her love of learning. She married Maxwell Phair, who studied the culture and languages of ancient Greece and Rome. Imagine the conversations they had! Venetia Burney Phair lived until the age of ninety. She died in Surrey, England, on April 30, 2009.

And what about Pluto? As telescopes became stronger, scientists found other icy, rocky objects in the outer reaches of the solar system where Pluto orbits. They named the region the Kuiper Belt. In 2005, an object that appeared to be larger than Pluto was discovered. The discovery of Eris, as it was named, led scientists to rethink the definition of a planet. In 2006, based on that new definition, scientists made the difficult decision to reclassify Pluto as a dwarf planet.

In an interview with NASA, when Venetia was asked whether she was upset by the decision, she responded, "I suppose I would prefer it to remain a planet."

Grandfather Madan understood the importance of Venetia's contribution to science. Along with his check to the school and his letter of thanks to Miss Claxton, he gave Venetia a five-pound note (worth more than three hundred dollars in today's currency) and two scrapbooks of articles about Venetia and Pluto that he'd clipped from newspapers.

Venetia is the only child to have named a planet, and science has honored her for it. In 2006, when NASA launched *New Horizons*—a robotic spacecraft that would fly to Pluto and beyond—on board was an instrument named the Venetia Burney Student Dust Counter. It was the first instrument on a NASA mission designed, built, and operated by students. When *New Horizons* reached Pluto in July 2015, it photographed a large crater-filled area there—which was named Burney Basin.

SELECTED BIBLIOGRAPHY

amblesideonline.org/PR/PR62p030PlanetPluto.shtml (Miss Claxton describing the planet walk; Grandfather's letter to Miss Claxton.)

Jimenez, Ginita, director. *Naming Pluto.* Father Films: 2008. (Documentary film.)

nasa.gov/multimedia/podcasting/transcript_pluto_naming_podcast.html (Interview, Venetia Burney Phair.)

"A New Planet," *The Times* [London, England], March 14, 1930. *The Times* Digital Archive. Accessed March 3, 2016. (Article that Grandfather Madan read in the *London Times,* shortened to fit the text.)

news.bbc.co.uk/2/hi/science/nature/4596246.stm ("The Girl Who Named a Planet," 2006.)

Moore, Patrick. "The Naming of Pluto," *Sky and Telescope*, November, 1984: 400–401. (Excerpts from the text of the telegram sent by Professor Herbert Hall Turner to Grandfather Madan.)

sci-news.com/space/new-horizons-highresolution-views-dwarf-planet-pluto-03492.html (NASA—Burney Basin, photo of Pluto.)